Milk & Honey WOMEN

DEVOTIONAL Journal

Vol. 1

WWW.MILKANDHONEYBOOKS.COM

SIGN UP ONLINE FOR FREE PRINTABLES AND MORE

Milk & Honey Women Devotional Journal Vol. 1

This book is available at: www.milkandhoneybooks.com and other online retailers

Reach us on the Internet: www.milkandhoneybooks.com
ISBN 13: 978-1-953000-08-8

For Worldwide Distribution

This Beauty Belongs to

Bonnie ♡

Contents

An Introduction

When was the last time you laughed? Really dug in deep to joy and held it so tight that tears pooled in the corners of your eyes, sides heaving for breath as you surrendered to delight?

When was the last time you were inspired, even in the midst of the mundane? Something washing over you so fresh and vibrant that you had to quickly grab a notebook to write down the creative solution to the problem you'd been praying through.

Or when was the last time you sat still, overcome so much by God's presence that all you could do was pause and rest in his love for you?
When was the last time?

Oftentimes those moments seem so elusive. As if we have to dig for them like treasure in some far off land that is nowhere near the place you find yourself in now. Maybe if we add it to the list of our responsibilities and To-Dos, we can make room for something that resembles what we crave at the core.

Know who I am in Christ? Check. I think.
Do my best to live a life of devotion? Check. I hope.
Delight myself in the Lord? Stir up the gift within me? Fan it into flame?
Che—Wait.
How do I live out the call on my life when any spark of delight, creativity, or rest is drowned out by the commotion of ever increasing responsibilities?
How can I even find the capacity to dream when I'm trying to just breathe?

Yes. There it is. Just breathe.
I'm here to tell you that you have permission to breathe. This is what I hope you hold in your hands. Simple reminders to position yourself in Christ, no matter what season you are in.

I hope this is a breath of fresh air as you read through and savor the Christ-centered voices of women who walk in shoes that are similar to yours. I am thankful for the words that pour out from leaders with public and visible platforms. The messages they carry have facilitated life-change and breakthrough for so many. So thankful! However, this does not take away the value of the woman next door, the sister in a hidden season, or the one who is publicly quiet but privately overflows with anointed wisdom. There is a seat at the table for women such as these and this is the core desire of Milk & Honey Women. As we cultivate our sweet spots of Christ-Centered Identity, Intimacy, and Influence in all areas, we want the call of God on our lives to encourage every woman.

From this devotional journal, we hope that you are stirred by the words of the women featured. Many times the simple encouragement of a friend is what you need to keep going. The strength from other sisters pushes you to pursue hope in what's to come, giving you the courage to pull up a chair to the table too.

As you go through each devotion, dig deeper into the Word of God, write down reflections, gratitude and prayer—we pray that sweet spots of God's presence are cultivated in your own life, in every season.

– *Jenny Erlingsson*
MILK & HONEY BOOKS
MILK & HONEY WOMEN

FOR MORE INFO ON MILK & HONEY WOMEN AND OTHER OPPORTUNITIES LIKE THIS ONE, HEAD TO WWW.MILKANDHONEYWOMEN.COM. ALSO, DON'T FORGET TO SIGN UP FOR OUR EMAIL LIST.

Wild Flowers Growing

Wild flowers are something to be seen.
They grow wherever their seed is carried.
Wherever the Lord decides to plant them.

Growing vibrant colors between concrete sidewalks.
Growing high up above the grasses to reach the sunlight.
Growing in hard and forgotten places.

Thriving despite its surroundings.

And they don't worry about how they'll bloom.
Or where they'll grow.
Or if they're good enough.
They continue to sow beauty, in the way they are told.

Their beauty goes beyond their petal.
They are resilience wrapped up in poise and grace.
They are unique from one another.
They hold their heads high and they know their place.

So look up, though the rains may pour.
The winds blow hard and you are shaken to the core.
Find rest in your waiting.
Send your roots down deep below.

One day you too will burst forth in brilliant colors.

No matter where you are planted.
Or the length it takes for you to see some growth.
Don't become weary in this season of struggle
Allowing worry to affect all you know.

Trust that He has not failed you,
but He has planted you in this place to thrive and grow.

—**Janessa Cypher**

*"Consider how the wild flowers
grow. They do not labor or spin.
Yet I tell you, not even Solomon in
all his splendor was dressed like one
of these."*
Luke 12:27 NIV

CLOTHED IN
Righteousness

> "I will greatly rejoice in the Lord; my soul shall exult in my God, for He has clothed me with the garments of salvation; He has covered me with the robe of righteousness… as a bride adorns herself with her jewels."
> Isaiah 61:10 ESV

You are clothed in righteousness.

Read that verse again.

Who is it that clothes us in salvation and righteousness? It's God, not us. I can picture a bride walking down the aisle to her groom, adorned in precious jewelry, with flowers in her hair, and a train of white following her every step.

Sigh.

Who doesn't love a good wedding? God compares this lovely bride as one who is clothed in righteousness and salvation. It's a beautiful thing to be clothed in those garments. If you are a Christian, a Jesus follower, this promise is for you. You are that beautiful bride, clothed in righteousness in God's eyes. He doesn't see that lie you told last week or that sarcastic comment you made to your husband, or even that gossip you started. He sees His garment of righteousness on your shoulders, and is ready to meet you at the end of the aisle.

Now that doesn't excuse us from giving into our sin struggles. God has given us the Holy Spirit to help us fight against our fleshly desires and live according to His Word (Romans 8:1-11). God expects us to obey Him as any child would obey their loving father. But when we mess up, because we will, He will forgive us and not let the robe of righteousness slip from our shoulders. He will remove those sins as far as the east is from the west (Psalm 103:12).

Clothed in Righteousness

We will be welcomed into the King's kingdom, clothed in the beautiful garments of salvation and righteousness, as a Bride coming home to her Beloved. Now that's a beautiful promise.

Prayer: Lord Jesus, I thank you for clothing me in righteousness. Especially because I don't deserve it. Thank you for always forgiving me and helping me with my sin struggle. Thank you for putting the Holy Spirit in me, who guides me and corrects me. Please help me live a righteous life in obedience. I love you, Amen.

Challenge: Read Romans 8:1-11. Now read it again. Highlight every time it says "Spirit" and "life".

—Ashley Djokoto

As you read, what promises mean the most to you in this season?

By God's sacrifice of His only son I am redeemed.

Further Reflection

Romans 8 1-11

If I belong to Christ Jesus (and I do)
I am free from condemnation. We are
weak in our sinful nature alone. In
Jesus I am made strong, forgiven for
my sinful nature.

God so loved us, despite this ever
present sinful nature that he gave
us his son in the flesh made like us
as a sacrifice. Why would he want
to sacrifice this only son? That is
a huge sacrifice and one I would
not want to make. He did this for
ALL of humanity. This means he
loves all of us.

Remaining in him leads to a life
of peace and tranquility for an
eternity. What are we willing to
sacrifice today for eternity?

Salvation & Righteousness

Salvation is defined as: preservation or deliverance from harm, ruin or loss. In theology it is deliverance from sin & its consequences, brought about by faith in Christ. Wow, what a deal!! Believe in Christ & be delivered from sin & it's consequences. Sounds too good to be true!!

Righteousness: the quality of being morally right or justifiable. "A right standing with God."

Again I question why God would do this? The only answer I can see is that he loves us so much he really wants to give us the benefit of the doubt.

I'm thankful for

my salvation and for the work that God continues to do in my sweet husband.

Lord, I'm asking you for

Protection for my family. Please keep them all safe physically & mentally. Soften Siomar's heart & teach him humility. I see his heart & his fear which causes him to hurt others.

And if the Spirit of him who raised Jesus from the dead is living in you, he who raised Christ from the dead will also give life to your mortal bodies because of his *Spirit* who lives in you.

Romans 8:11 NIV

THE ONE WHO Sees Me

> "Let us then approach the throne of grace with confidence, that we may receive mercy and find grace to help us in our time of need."
> Hebrews 4:16 NIV

It happened in slow motion.

The words marched out of her mouth and onto the table, covering our food and our friendship. I went numb, stumbling through the remnants of a conversation as my mind tried to make sense of what had happened. It was only after I was home and safely behind closed doors that the hurt sunk in. I had been blindsided and wounded by a dear friend and sister in Christ. In the pain of it, every fear and doubt and insecurity I ever had, raised it's ugly head. "She was never your friend. You are alone."

I wonder if you've ever found yourself in a similar place? If you've ever been hurt by the actions or words of a loved one? If you've ever been assailed by fears and insecurities? What do you do in those moments? Where do you turn?

All too often I run for comfort or distraction (block of chocolate and Netflix, anyone?). But those things do nothing to heal the pain or bring about change. I desperately need a hope and a truth that I can hold onto. I need to know that I am not alone, that there is someone who sees me and understands.

What a precious thing it is to find that in Christ Jesus!

In Him, I find a Friend who is familiar with suffering (Isaiah 53:3) and who can sympathize fully with the pain I feel. My hurt came in the intimacy of a meal with a friend, His was in a kiss. Mine was one friend, yet all of His disciples deserted Him (Matthew 26:47-56). Surely He was tempted to anger and bitterness, just as I was.

In Him, I find a Great High Priest who gently, lovingly teaches me how to respond and intercedes for me. He has suffered, He has been betrayed, He has been alone.

Because of me. For me.
Because of you. For you.

In His great love, He chose these things so that when we are in Him, we will never be alone and we will never receive what our sins deserve. Instead, we can draw near to the true and constant Savior and Friend whose mercy and grace are more than enough.

That day, as I poured out my heart to my Friend, I found precious and real comfort. I rested in the One who sees me.

— Rachel Mutesi

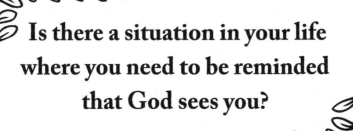

Is there a situation in your life where you need to be reminded that God sees you?

Further Reflection

Recently my good friend, who supported and loved me through all that I went through with George, really disappointed me. She decided not to come with me on a vacation and I was very hurt & disappointed I felt she had -○- loyalty to me. She chose staying home to be with her short term boyfriend over me. Or this is how I saw it at the time. This may not be entirely accurate. It's not all about me!! She has her own agenda and host of insecurities. I really don't think this was personal in retro-spect.

She has her own issues to deal with and I have mine. It is not personal.

I'm thankful for

Lord, I'm asking you for

....

....

....

....

....

....

She gave this name to the LORD who spoke to her: "You are the God who sees me," for she said, "I have now seen the One who *Sees* me.

Genesis 16:13 NIV

INTERNAL
Identity

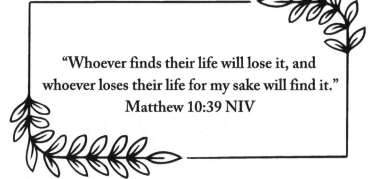

> "Whoever finds their life will lose it, and whoever loses their life for my sake will find it."
> Matthew 10:39 NIV

God is teaching me that my identity is not what I thought it was.

Work, ministry, volunteer, and church titles used to define me. These titles pointed towards what I did, but not who I am.

Identity has to be more than a career, church, or civic affiliation.

It is both internal and eternal.

The body has limitations but the spirit lives on forever. If my identity is based on something external, the moment things change (which they always do) I find myself in an identity crisis.

Unexpected crises are often the catalyst that helps me find my way back to Christ. Catastrophe has the ability to reveal who I am by highlighting who I am not.

If you've ever lost a job, had a long-term relationship come to an end, experienced hurt while serving in ministry, been falsely accused, or been betrayed by a close friend, you likely received a crash course lesson in how intimate, intricate, and internal identity is.

When your world comes crashing down, what holds you together?

When the guilt, shame, anger, or pain of a bad choice floods your soul with condemnation, what compels you to keep moving forward? That's who you are? Or perhaps I should say, "That's whose you are."

Identity is as simple as it is complex, and it always starts within. If you feel far away from who you thought you would become, you are probably closer to being who God created you to be.

— **Toya Poplar**

What truth do you need to agree with today, to replace the lies that you have once believed?

Further Reflection

Internal Identity

....

....

....

....

....

....

....

....

....

....

....

....

....

....

....

....

....

....

....

....

....

....

....

....

....

I'm thankful for

Lord, I'm asking you for

....

....

....

....

....

....

For you died, and your life is now *Hidden* with Christ in God.

Colossians 3:3 NIV

SEEING WHAT
God Sees

Wild flowers are something to be seen. You formed my innermost being, shaping my delicate inside and my intricate outside, and wove them all together in my mother's womb.
Psalm 139:14 TPT

Pain, trauma and shame will often blur the lens of our identity.

These experiences can make it hard to differentiate from who we are in the eyes of God versus what we have been through in our lives.

The beautiful thing about God is if we choose to bring Him every weight of false identity we have been carrying, we can begin the great exchange with Him.

When we believe that our identity is attached to what we have been through, what we do, or our social status, the moments we spend with God bring the necessary light for us to see clearly.

We see that He never intended for us to view ourselves this way.

This is where we give Him all our burdens and false beliefs, in exchange for his love and healing.

It is only the love of our heavenly Father that can take everything designed to break us down and instead use it to restore us, cultivate us, and bring us closer to Him.

The more time we spend in His presence we become free to see ourselves through His eyes. Even just a glimpse of seeing what He sees in us will forever change us.

As we become intentional in sharing more and more quiet moments with our Heavenly Father we will begin to see the beauty of the story He has written for us.

Our eyes are opened to see that our identity was never associated with the false standards of "worth" we held for ourselves or even allowed society to place on us.

As we continue to open our hearts to God, we will dive deeper into His heart for us. The closer we get to Him, we see that every fabric of our being was created with love, intention, and purpose.

—Erin Elise

How is the Lord opening your eyes to see yourself more clearly?

Further Reflection

I'm thankful for

Lord, I'm asking you for

....

....

....

....

....

....

I thank you, God, for making me so mysteriously complex! Everything you do is marvelously breathtaking. It simply amazes me to think about it! How thoroughly you *know* me, Lord!

Psalm 119:14 TPT

Walking in *the Dark*

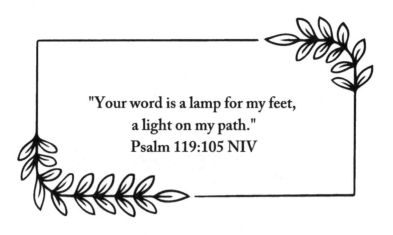

> "Your word is a lamp for my feet,
> a light on my path."
> Psalm 119:105 NIV

Have you ever had to walk in the dark before? Even in a familiar place, it can be very disorienting.

Our 2nd child has a life-threatening disease that we have to monitor every hour of every day. It's become second nature to our lives right now, but it's still challenging at times.

In the middle of the night we sometimes have to get up to check on him and wake him to eat. I have an amazing husband who does this most of the time, although there are nights that I trade with him. I am normally a heavy sleeper so if anything wakes me, I consider that unusual.

A couple of weeks ago I woke up out of the blue. I laid in bed and prayed, asking the Lord what He was speaking to me. But I wasn't able to go back to sleep. Then I thought, I need to check on Silas (our son). So, I got up out of the bed and walked from one end of the house to the other to get to his bedroom. I couldn't see a thing. It was pitch black. Yet, I walked straight through without a problem. I got to his bedroom, made sure he was okay and then had enough peace to head back to my room to go back to sleep.

On the way back to our end of the house, I started thinking about how wild it was that I could make it straight through the house without bumping into anything. Even though I couldn't see, I stayed on the familiar path as I walked back to my bedroom.

Walking in the Dark

I have firm memories of the solid structures in my home, I know how to maneuver around them even if I can't see them. The key is that I don't veer to the right or the left when I'm in the dark. I trust what I know is solid and foundational, and I stick with the path I know.

I can't help but think of the darkness we are living in these days. The unknown paths we are all on. Just like when I was walking through my dark house, we have to stay on what we know is true, solid and unmovable.

We can't "doubt in the dark what God has told us in the light" (Amazing lyrics to a song by Rita Springer)

We have to stick to the firm foundation of God's words and promises. In these days, when you're feeling weary, lost, and in the dark, hold tight to all the things you know are stationary, firm and true! Do not veer to the left or the right. Stick to the path that you are familiar with and don't doubt. Morning will come and we will see clearly again.

— Buffi Young

What are some of the promises God has given you that you need to remember in dark places?

Further Reflection

I'm thankful for

Lord, I'm asking you for

....

....

....

....

....

....

Even though I walk through the darkest valley, I will fear no evil, for you are with me; your rod and your staff, they *Comfort* me.

Psalm 23:4 NIV

SHARE THE
Burden

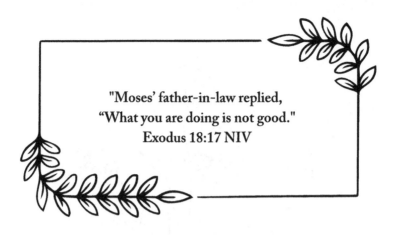

"Moses' father-in-law replied,
"What you are doing is not good."
Exodus 18:17 NIV

Instead of picking up the Legos scattered across the floor, while my daughter napped, I sat down and finished the watercolor painting she had asked me to complete.

I am not a super artsy person. I prefer to paint with words then with colors, but there was something rejuvenating in quietly mixing reds and oranges to finish a sunset on that simple watercolor. When I finished, I had a much better attitude about tackling the mess of toys and the pile of dirty dishes.

Sometimes the pull of never-ending work can leave such dryness. That is where Jethro, found Moses, teetering on the edge of burnout. Doing good things, but holding too much of a burden that needed to be shared. "Why do you sit alone, and all the people stand around you from morning till evening" he asked his son-in-law (Exodus 18:14). "Because the people come to me to inquire of God" Moses responded (Exodus 18:15). "You and the people with you will completely wear yourselves out, for the thing is too heavy for you" Jethro wisely remarked (Exodus 18:18).

To his credit, Moses listened. He began to let others carry the burden with him appointing judges to hear more simple cases and only tackling the complicated ones.

It is so easy to take on more then you are meant to carry. For a while you might manage, but I have had to learn the hard way that if something is meant to be sustainable you have to let others carry the burden with you.

For me, that has meant putting my kiddos in school part-time so that I have more time to focus on ministry, writing and the callings that God has placed on my heart. Of course, raising children is an important piece of that. But at times I have bought into the lie that only I can do that properly, instead of leaning on the talented community that surrounds me and can help me carry this beautiful burden.

I am also learning the importance of taking time out to do creative things that feed my soul, so that I can engage in the work that is before me with an attitude of joy and not one of duty. Because when one works from a posture of joy, not of duty, the offering is so much sweeter.

— Ruth Potinu

How can you position yourself to work from a posture of collaboration and joy?

Further Reflection

Share the Burden

....
....
....
....
....
....
....
....
....
....
....
....
....
....
....
....
....
....
....
....
....
....
....
....
....

I'm thankful for

Lord, I'm asking you for

....

....

....

....

....

....

Carry **each other's burdens, and in this way you will fulfill the law of Christ.**

Galatians 6:2 NIV

GOD HONORS
Our Integrity

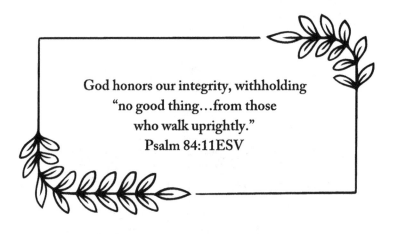

God honors our integrity, withholding
"no good thing…from those
who walk uprightly."
Psalm 84:11ESV

I love Hannah's story. So much of it bears some semblance to life today—

The deep-seeded desire of a woman;
the taunting mean girl;
the husband who imprudently attempts to fix his wife's longing;
the onlooker who sees the outside of a person and makes hurried assumptions;
and the God who so compassionately sees.

But beyond her story, there is something about Hannah that makes me take a second and third and fourth look at her.
Something that caused her to walk securely in her faith (Proverbs 10:9).
Something that assured her that God was her shield (Proverbs 2:7).
Something that upheld her and set her in God's presence forever (Psalm 41:11-12).
Something, this depraved world needs a lot more of—and that's integrity.

See, year after heartbreaking year, Hannah took the taunting and the misunderstanding and the false indictments and did this with them:

"In the bitterness of soul Hannah wept much and prayed to the Lord. And she made a vow saying, "O Lord Almighty, if you will only look upon your servant's misery and remember me, and not forget your servant but give her a son, then I will give him to the Lord for all the days of his life, and no razor will ever be used on his head." (1 Samuel 1:10-11)

Scripture tells us that Hannah wept much, revealing her humanity.

She prayed to the Lord, reflecting her humility.

And Hannah made a vow—a vow that would test the heart-strings of any mother – yet, she didn't waver. Both human and humble, she made her vow to God from a posture of utter desperation and she kept that vow revealing a posture of utmost faith.

As a consequence, God rewarded her integrity. 1 Samuel tell us that the Lord was gracious to Hannah. Some translations say that He "visited" her, opening her womb five more times to bare three sons and two daughters.

Indeed, Hannah's story reminds us that our tears matter to God. Our prayers matter to God. The vows we make, while praying, matter to God. And the vows we keep matter to God. He honors our integrity, not just for us, but, like Hannah, for the generation that follows.

— Stephanie Prater-Clarke

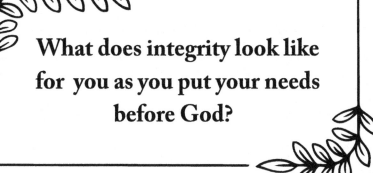

What does integrity look like for you as you put your needs before God?

Further Reflection

God Honors Our Integrity

....
....
....
....
....
....
....
....
....
....
....
....
....
....
....
....
....
....
....
....
....
....
....
....
....

I'm thankful for

Lord, I'm asking you for

....

....

....

....

....

....

Some trust in chariots and some in horses, but we *trust* in the name of the Lord our God.

Psalm 20:7 ESV

NEVER
Abandoned

I will not leave you as orphans;
I will come to you.
John 14:18 NIV

Father God has been doing some serious inner healing work in my life/heart over the last few years.

One root that came to the surface of my heart was a deep desire for His approval and acceptance. I'll never forget the prophetic words, inspired by the Holy Spirit, that were spoken over me at a conference I attended in Georgia several summers ago. That individual who spoke over me saw a picture of me on a treadmill. The treadmill was on the steepest incline and on the highest speed and I was running my little heart out! That picture described my relationship with the Father.

Me working. Me trying. Me stressing. Me working to gain His acceptance.

Me striving to gain His approval. Me wanting Him to be proud of me but always feeling like I was failing. Why didn't I feel accepted? Why did I feel like I needed to earn God's love and approval?

You see, I grew up fatherless. I never had a relationship with my biological father or his side of the family. All of my mother's family lived in the northeastern part of the country. We lived in the south so there was little relationship that took place between us. However, the Lord was so faithful to put people in my life that loved me and took care of me even though there was no blood relation. But somewhere along the way there was a lie planted deep in my heart that I didn't really belong anywhere.

When I was a sophomore in college that lie of abandonment deepened when my mom moved up north to be closer to her aging mother. I was alone. I had to fend for and care for myself. I felt abandoned and displaced. But was I really? As the Lord, in His goodness and faithfulness, began to tear down the lies of abandonment and displacement in my life, I began to crave more and more intimacy with Him.

As I did, Milk and Honey in the Land of Fire & Ice taught me that as my identity as a daughter comes into greater and greater alignment, my intimacy with Father will go deeper and deeper. Identity and intimacy are directly correlated. Consequently, my desire for more intimacy has helped me walk in a greater fullness of who I am as His daughter.

— Dasha Sigurmundsson

Has there been past rejection in your life that has affected how you respond in certain situations?

Further Reflection

....
....
....
....
....
....
....
....
....
....
....
....
....
....
....
....
....
....
....
....
....
....
....
....

I'm thankful for

Lord, I'm asking you for

....
....
....
....
....
....

And surely I am with you

to the very end of the age.

Matthew 28:20b NIV

THE WAR
For Us

> "For there is one God, and there is one mediator between God and men, the man, Christ Jesus, who gave himself as a ransom for all, which is the testimony given at the proper time."
> 1 Timothy 2:5-6 NIV

The war was fierce and futile as created ones rebelled against Creator.

Holy and just, the Creator King beheld his people standing in enmity toward Him with sadness, but without surprise. He knew each one of them completely.

Knew every molecule of their being, every hair on their head, every thought in their mind, the tears and the joys and every moment marked out for them. Each person unique and precious, made in His own image, a beloved work of art. He knew each one completely, and He knew rebellion would come.

A war is won in the shedding of blood. This war, this rebellion, had created a deep and terrible rift which separated the people from the Creator, from life itself. The created ones had won for themselves nothing but death, just wrath and condemnation, and they had no way back.

But the just Creator King was also rich in mercy and grace. Before time began, He knew that this would happen. Before time began, He had a plan.

The Son went gladly, compelled by love for His creation and a delight to do the will of the Father. It was no small thing. The holy, Uncreated One, became created, and dwelt with the rebellious ones.

He lived for them and died for them, taking their place so that they might live. In His outstretched arms and blood poured out He took His place between the warring sides and at great cost He brokered peace.

How often I take for granted this wonderful story! Filled with love and war, terrible sacrifice, amazing grace, when I stop to contemplate what God has done I am filled with awe and gratitude. Christ Jesus mediates for me, and in Him, I have life eternal and everlasting peace.

— Rachel Mutesi

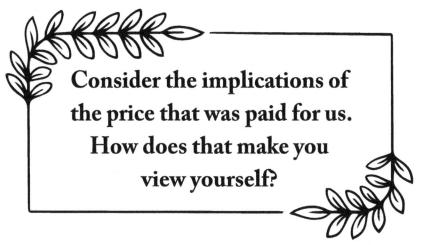

Consider the implications of the price that was paid for us. How does that make you view yourself?

Further Reflection

I'm thankful for

Lord, I'm asking you for

....

....

....

....

....

....

But now he has reconciled you by Christ's physical body through death to present you holy in his sight, without blemish and *Free* from accusation. **Colossians 1:22 NIV**

Beautiful Things

Beautiful things take time.
Consider a flower.
It doesn't just spring up and bloom.

There is a growing. A giving.
A learning of what to do.

What begins as a tiny seed must first let go and die.
Down in the deep, dark and unknown
for it to fully come alive.

It waits. Then it starts to shake.
And something breaks forth.

Ever tiny roots shoot out as a tiny sprout springs up.
Towards the surface. Towards the light.
Not to escape the deep darkness, but anchor itself
To hold on tight.

For tiny roots from a once tiny seed,
provide a foundation for it to grow.
This often isn't a fast process.
It's often incredibly slow.

Until the ground begins to rumble
with life about to break through.

It's hard.
It's painful.
But worth the wait for those blooms
to blossom in you.

Can you hear the sound of dirt cracking,
making space for a tiny sprout to break through?

It will happen one day,
even though all you feel is darkness.

When you are surrounded by uncertainty,
this growing process holds true.

Trust Him in the waiting.

It will happen beautiful one,
This is the process.
And it will certainly happen for you.

—Janessa Cypher

CHOOSING *Thanksgiving*

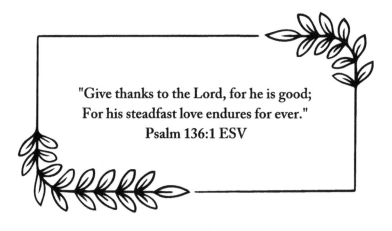

"Give thanks to the Lord, for he is good;
For his steadfast love endures for ever."
Psalm 136:1 ESV

I find myself having to learn the same spiritual truths over and over again.

When faced with challenges, I am often tempted towards despondency. As a writer, I regularly feel frustrated and blocked. Whenever I feel low, I invariably get the advice: 'Count your blessings'. I am not always good at accepting this as encouragement. I have a small tantrum, then consider God's blessings, and find that it does help to change my perspective.

Similarly, with writer's block, there is much advice out there. What helps me is the notion of 'creative play'. This takes away the pressure of writing for an audience. It is a return to the pure enjoyment of creating. I still tend to sit staring at a blank page, willing myself to create. But when I seek inspiration by using a prompt, however simplistic the exercise might seem, I am rewarded with the joy of using my creativity.

This devotion combines these ideas. Following Psalm 136 as a model and prompt, write your own list-poem of thanksgiving to God. You are not writing for publication or a wider audience, just using your creativity to enjoy time with God.

Psalm 136 has the refrain, 'His love endures forever'. You might also use this. If there is another characteristic of God that you want to emphasize, you could use that instead, for example, 'His mercies are new every morning'. The psalm starts with an exhortation to give thanks to God, 'for he is good', before reminding us who we're praising: 'the God of gods' and 'the Lord of lords' (v 1-3). It describes God's deeds, starting with creation.

Choosing Thanksgiving

The psalmist recalls ways in which God has shown love to his people. Specific details are given, such as God's defeat of 'Sihon king of the Amorites' and 'Og king of Bashan' (v 19, 20). I love the contrasting perspectives, from the God who created the universe, to the One who is present in every battle we face. You could write about your own experiences, reminding yourself that God's love carries you through every circumstance.

Here's my psalm, "Choosing Thanksgiving".

I will give thanks to you God,
Your love endures forever.
Thank you, God, you are always good,
Your love endures forever.
You created galaxies from nothing,
Your love endures forever,
And you made us from the dust,
Your love endures forever.
You have given me family,
Your love endures forever,
I know I am never alone,
Your love endures forever.
You give me a voice and a purpose
Your love endures for ever,
You make me a co-labourer with you
Your love endures forever.
You are writing me into your story,
Your love endures for ever
You are the beginning and the end,
Your love endures forever.

— **Naomi Marklew**

Further Reflection

Choosing Thanksgiving

....
....
....
....
....
....
....
....
....
....
....
....
....
....
....
....
....
....
....
....
....
....
....
....
....
....

I'm thankful for

Lord, I'm asking you for

....

....

....

....

....

....

Give thanks to the God of heaven. His love *Endures* forever.

Psalm 136:26 NIV

BEAUTIFUL
In time

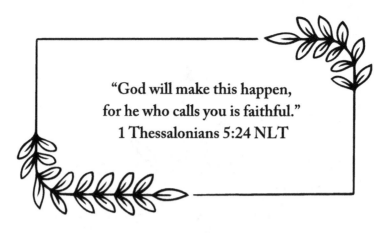

> "God will make this happen,
> for he who calls you is faithful."
> 1 Thessalonians 5:24 NLT

Did you know that a pearl is formed from an oyster, mussel or clam?

When a parasite works its way into the clam, the clam produces a coat that is used to irritate the parasite. Layers form and in time, a pearl develops. That ugly, slimy clam produces something beautiful and expensive.

Sometimes, I wonder how God could keep loving me when I mess up so many times. Sometimes I even think my heart must look ugly to God. But that's the thing. Even though God hates sin and hates that we choose to sin against Him, He's turning our sinful hearts to Him day by day. He's making our dirty, sin loving hearts and cleaning them, making them pure and holy – like Himself.

"For God knew his people in advance, and he chose them to become like his Son, so that his Son would be the firstborn among many [sisters]." Romans 8:29

God chose you and I to become like His Son, holy and blameless. Beautiful and pure before Him. It's a process. It doesn't come right away, but will take a lifetime—literally. And it's not always easy. Most of the time it's hard and painful. Much like that parasite must be to the clam.

I don't know about you, but I would be resentful if a little parasite came knocking on my door, taking up space in my home, and rubbing against me night and day. No wonder they try to protect themselves with slime.

But really, the same happens with us.

Minus the slime part.

Becoming like Jesus is not easy. Sometimes it seems impossible. But the beautiful thing is that it's not up to us – it's God who is doing the work within us, and He will continue until we are beautiful and like Him completely.

Challenge: Start keeping a journal and write down the ways you see God working in your life. In a month, go back and reread what you wrote. I promise, it's amazing and super encouraging to be reminded of what God has done in your life. It's often not until you walk through something that you can look back and see what God did in you and through you. Be encouraged! God is faithful.

— Ashley Djokoto

How have you seen God work in your life this week? This month?

Further Reflection

I'm thankful for

Lord, I'm asking you for

....

....

....

....

....

....

He has made
everything

Beautiful

in its time.

Ecclesiastes 3:11a NIV

A Heart For *Home*

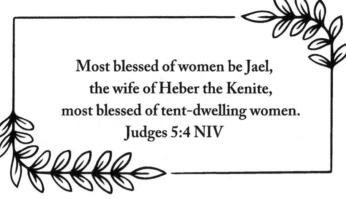

Most blessed of women be Jael,
the wife of Heber the Kenite,
most blessed of tent-dwelling women.
Judges 5:4 NIV

I didn't dream a lot as a kid.

I don't even recall any memories of what I wanted to be when I grew up. In my adulthood, the fact that I didn't dream bothered me.

One day I was in fellowship with the Lord and He reminded that I did, in fact, have a dream as a young adult. Growing up in fatherlessness and brokenness, my dream was for my future children to have a father. I wanted a healthy marriage and a husband who loved me deeply.

I wanted my children to have all the things that I lacked growing up: a father's presence, a mother who didn't have to work so hard and could be present, a healthy, whole family that followed hard after God.

After He reminded me of this dream, He told me that He had fulfilled this longing in my life.

It was true! I was living my dream, but up until that point hadn't realized it. The Lord knows me so intimately that He fulfilled the deepest desire of my heart before I even remembered my dream from long ago.

But somewhere along the way I bought into a lie that being a mom and a wife wasn't enough. I was often plagued with thoughts of feeling like I needed to go back to work. Like I wasn't doing enough for my family or the Kingdom. I felt purposeless.

Finally, the Lord in the sweetest way, broke the situation all the way down for me. During my the reading of Milk & Honey in the Land of Fire & Ice, He confirmed and affirmed in my heart that I am, in fact, a Jael of sorts (Judges 4 & 5).

My heart is for the home. That pleases Him.

I have a call to live simply and to love my husband and children well. That pleases Him.

My role as a homemaker is valuable. He is proud of me!

Mother Theresa's words continue to ring so loudly in my heart— "I can change the world by loving my family". As unbelievable as it sounds, I know it's true.

— Dasha Sigurmundson

What is your dream? How has that been fulfilled (even partially) in your life?

Further Reflection

I'm thankful for

Lord, I'm asking you for

....

....

....

....

....

....

I arose, a *Mother* in Israel

Judges 5:7b NIV

THE BLACK
Shirt

> So here's what I want you to do, God helping you:
> Take your everyday, ordinary life—your sleeping,
> eating, going-to-work, and walking-around life—and
> place it before God as an offering...
> Romans 12:1-2 MSG

Ok, I have a confession.

A few years ago I purchased a black shirt from a second hand store. I loved it! It was made from polyester and didn't wrinkle or anything. It became my favorite shirt. The bad thing is...after almost 10 years...it is still my favorite shirt and my husband begs me not to wear it anymore.

I know that we all have our favorite things that we like to put on, but I believe that I took this black shirt to a new level. I could literally wear it everyday of the week. One morning, I found myself putting it on again and I wondered "why in the world do I wear this all the time?"

First, it was comfortable. I felt that to some degree it looked nice just in case I had to go out unexpectedly. Second, it took no thought to figure out what to wear. I didn't and still don't like having to put forth effort into worrying about what to wear each day. Lastly, it was a habit. Something I had gotten used to doing for almost the last decade...and it was just, plain comfortable for me to do.

When I began to think about this, I thought to myself, "This really can't be a good thing. My hubby is right." Wear something different...don't stay in the same old rut. Yes, I'm talking about clothes but this can be applied to life in general. What do we do when we get into what I call a "funk" a "rut"? We revert to our old, comfortable way of doing things. Which most of the time, isn't good for us.

The Black Shirt

It's just easier to do things the way we used to or the way that is comfortable. It's WORK to change the way we look at certain situations, or what we choose to do with our days, or how we respond to different circumstances. It's just plain uncomfortable to step out of our routine and do something different, isn't it? But our old ways need to be renewed and refined.

In the book of Romans, it talks about not doing things in the same pattern as the world. We can look at "the world" as the secular things out there. But we can also look at it as the way we do things in "our little world". Those comfortable habits become easy things that require no thought or effort on our part. The little "ruts" that we get into.

Consider the verse shared at the beginning. The key is "God helping You". To fix our attention on Him and the way He wants us to respond and what He wants us to do. After all...isn't that the best way? Even in small things. Like the way I don't like to think about what I'm going to wear. It's a rut...a negative way for me to think and I just need to daily ask God to help me so I can finally lay this black shirt down.

What's the black shirt in your life today? What do you pick up on a daily basis that is maybe a bad way of thinking....a negative, selfish action, a careless flippant way of living? We've all got to lay our comfortable "black shirts" down, and be challenged to choose a new way of looking at life.

— Buffi Young

...Embracing what God does for you is the best thing you can do for him. Don't become so well-adjusted to your culture that you fit into it without even thinking. Instead, fix your attention on God. You'll be changed from the inside out. Readily recognize what he wants from you, and quickly respond to it. Unlike the culture around you, always dragging you down to its level of immaturity...
Romans 12:1–2MSG

Further Reflection

....
....
....
....
....
....
....
....
....
....
....
....
....
....
....
....
....
....
....
....
....
....
....
....
....

I'm thankful for

Lord, I'm asking you for

....

....

....

....

....

....

God brings the Best out of you, develops well-formed maturity in you.

Romans 12:1-2 MSG

THE
Climb

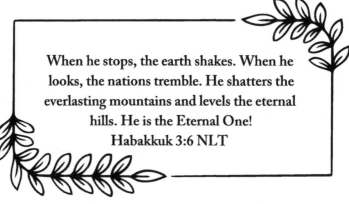

> When he stops, the earth shakes. When he looks, the nations tremble. He shatters the everlasting mountains and levels the eternal hills. He is the Eternal One!
> Habakkuk 3:6 NLT

Are you tired of this fast paced, work harder, never enough lifestyle we, especially as women, often find ourselves reaching for and even grasping to obtain?

It seems as if we are always scouring the horizon for the next best thing, or climbing the mountains of our lives as if our actual life depended on us reaching the summit. And often, when we don't get that job, lose those ten pounds, drive that car, take that vacation, or post the perfect story on social media, we view ourselves as failures. But, we must remember that God never once, not even for a second, put us on this Earth to achieve or accomplish. He put us here to live and to love, not just others but ourselves.

He planted us here to grow and to flourish.

Will we have struggles and adversities while we climb our way through life? Yes.
Will we have seasons in our lives when we feel scared, lonely, weak and weary? Yes.
Does God use the bad for good? Yes.

He is the one that goes before us and beside us, holding our hands.
He turns messes into messages and tests into testimonies.
We are never out of His reach.

So I challenge us to hit the stop button. Stop performing, perfecting, and pleasing. I encourage us to just be where we are; be who we are. Let's save ourselves mental anguish and emotional energy. Let's stop reaching for something different, something better. Let's speak, and live, and love from where we are right now. Right where God has planted us.

What do we do next? Let's just do the next best thing, the next right thing, the thing that's right in front of us. Instead of carrying the mountain of life, let's climb it one beautiful step at a time. If we stop carrying the mountain, and instead look around and inhale the beauty, inhale the mess, and inhale the hard work that is the climb; the view at the top will be that much more rewarding. It will be breathtakingly beautiful.

It is in and during the climb that God is teaching us, guiding us, leading us, transforming and restoring us. So, my friend, we can stop being the one doing all the reaching because our Savior's hand is guiding us all the way up the mountain. He is reaching down from Heaven, so let's enjoy the climb!

— Jodi Kinasewitz

> **What is the next best thing, the next right thing that you can do on your climb?**

Further Reflection

I'm thankful for

Lord, I'm asking you for

....

....

....

....

....

....

The mountains quake before him and the hills melt away. The earth trembles at his *presence* the world and all who live in it.

Nahum 1:5 NIV

WAITING
Well

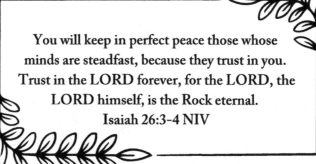

> You will keep in perfect peace those whose minds are steadfast, because they trust in you. Trust in the LORD forever, for the LORD, the LORD himself, is the Rock eternal.
> Isaiah 26:3-4 NIV

How do you catch your breath when disappointment brings you to your knees?
How do you grieve what is lost and move forward?
How do you hold both the deep pain and the hope that this isn't the end?

We recently went to court for the adoption of our two children. It didn't go well. We left feeling like the wind was knocked out of us. Everything that could have gone wrong did and we were left not knowing which pieces to pick up first.

And then came the wrestling.
The realization that the wait would be a little longer.

The paperwork wasn't close to being over. We were still stuck in this place of uncertainty, now left with only God to cling to.

Those tears hidden behind my mask in the courtroom threatened to release in full force. Years built up for this moment. We had been in this process for two years and we were so close to the end. So close to being a family. But we weren't at a stand still anymore. We had been significantly set back.

Life will knock you down.
The answer you are praying for doesn't come, and there are so many questions you are left with.
The unbearable weight of grief and hopelessness can threaten to break you.
And you are left holding it all.

On our drive home and still processing the morning's disappointments, I felt a stirring of two options before me. To wait these next months out in a deep frustration, allowing despair to overwhelm my daily living and taint my view of God's goodness. Or to wait this time out well, regardless of having no end in sight, by pushing through this hard place.

What would it look like to dig in and remain steadfast in the Lord's calling on your life? To press in harder when you have nothing left to give?
To rest in the surety and security of the Lord, despite the circumstances?

Are you willing to wait with open hands or clenched fists?

Let us hold tightly to the One who is the constant in our chaos and crisis.
Let us rest assured that he is working even this out for our good and His glory. Let us cling to hope and trust in His faithfulness.

And let us wait it out well.

—**Janessa Cypher**

How can you wait well in the midst of disappointments or as you anticipate something good?

Further Reflection

....

....

....

....

....

....

....

....

....

....

....

....

....

....

....

....

....

....

....

....

....

....

....

....

....

....

I'm thankful for

Lord, I'm asking you for

....

....

....

....

....

....

Let us hold fast the confession of our hope without wavering, for he who promised is *faithful*

Hebrews 10:23 ESV

LIVING FOR GOD'S
Pleasure

> I have filled him with the Spirit of God, with wisdom, with understanding, with knowledge and with all kinds of skills—to make artistic designs for work in gold, silver and bronze,
> Exodus 31:3-4 NIV

My favorite scene in the movie Chariots of Fire is when Eric Liddell tells his concerned sister that he has decided to go to China as a missionary.

"But," he clarifies. "I've got a lot of running to do first. Jenny, Jenny you've got to understand I believe that God made me for a purpose—for China. He also made me fast, and when I run, I feel His pleasure. To give it up would be to hold Him in contempt. You were right. It's not just fun. To win is to honor Him."

Liddell did continue to run, winning a gold medal in the 1924 Olympics. A win that surprised many as it was not the 100 meter race that Liddell had originally trained for, but the 400 meter race. A last minute switch that was made when Liddell refused to run in the 100 meter heats because they were held on Sunday.

Do you feel God's pleasure when you bake a birthday cake for a friend, when you write an inspirational Instagram post, when you share nuggets of truth with a classroom full of high school students? What is your sweet spot of, "this is my purpose. I can feel God's pleasure in this moment?"

I love Matthew 3:17 when the Father looks down on the Son fulfilling His earthly mission and says, "This is my, Son, whom I love; with him I am well pleased." When we walk in our God-given calling we bring God pleasure.

The beauty of this diverse body is that we are all created differently but all created to bring glory to the ultimate Creator. As John Piper famously puts it, "God is most glorified in us when we are most satisfied in Him." There is satisfaction in living out the gifts that God has placed inside of you, but it is even more than that. Using your gifts glorifies the One who placed those very gifts inside of you.

These gifts are not just gifts of teaching or preaching but also gifts of artful expression. Like the gift Bezalel was given in Exodus 31:2-4. The Holy Spirit especially gifted him, "in all manner of workmanship, to design artistic works" in order to build the tabernacle. Do not downplay the creative gifts God has placed in you. Run with them—and feel His pleasure as you do.

— Ruth Potinu

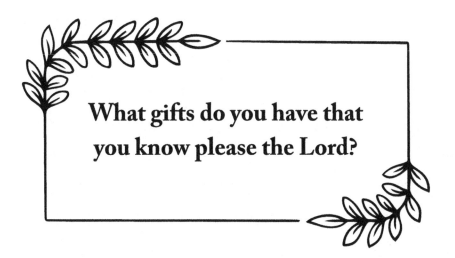

What gifts do you have that you know please the Lord?

Further Reflection

....

....

....

....

....

....

....

....

....

....

....

....

....

....

....

....

....

....

....

....

....

....

....

....

....

I'm thankful for

Lord, I'm asking you for

....

....

....

....

....

....

And a voice from heaven said, "This is my Son, whom I love; with him I am well *pleased*"

Matthew 3:17 NIV

Almond Tree

All is quiet and all growing slow.
Hope buried deep below the surface.

Waiting.

Yet, a branch starts shaking.
Soft white petals, flecks of pink begin to show
and a tiny bud starts to emerge, despite the season of
dark and cold.

When all is dormant in the hoping,
the bareness becomes beauty unfolding.
A promise that there is more to come.
There in the tiny bud of an almond tree.

To hold on.
To wait.
To watch.
To see.

He is making a way in the valley and in the unseen.
His faithfulness is plenty.
There in the tiny bud of an almond tree.

Then snow melts and cold hides away.
Green grows up all around, the sun and rain bring to
life all that grows.

But now there is a waiting.

While others start with the budding,
those blossoms continue to grow.
And soon the almond tree is left waiting with the
promise of more to come.
But as other trees begin to bear more and more fruit,
There is a shaking down deep within its roots.
Despite the early bud of an almond tree.

Then once the season of bearing and growing
seems to now be over,
the watching and waiting becomes consumed
with a showing.

The seed hidden finally come into fruition.
And a promise unfolds.

A trusting.
A hoping.
A revealing
A showing.

There despite the long waiting
in the once tiny bud of an almond tree.

—Janessa Cypher

*"The word of the Lord came to me: "What do you see,
Jeremiah?" "I see the branch of an almond tree," I replied.
The Lord said to me, "You have seen correctly, for I am
watching to see that my word is fulfilled."
Jeremiah 1:11–12 NIV*

WHO DO YOU
Influence?

> "But he, full of the Holy Spirit, gazed into heaven and saw the glory of God, and Jesus standing the right hand of God. And he said, "Behold, I see the heavens opened, and the Son of Man standing at the right hand of God."
> Acts 7:55-56 ESV

Everyone wants to be an influencer.

All our motivations are different but one of the downsides to being an influencer is dealing with the negativity that gets hurled your way. It's not for the faint at heart. Deep down, we all want to be influencers in some way because we all feel like we have something to say. The truth is we do have something to say when it comes to the God we serve, love and know.

But an important question to ask yourself is: who are you trying to influence?

Way before Instagram and TikTok, Stephen was an influencer. He was known among his people and was described in the Word of God as a man full of faith and of the Holy Spirit (Acts 6:5). He was chosen from among the people. Stephen was a man full of God's grace and power, and he performed great wonders and signs among the people.

However, Acts 6:9 says the two words no influencer ever wants to hear… OPPOSITION AROSE. Stephen was about to get cancelled. Suddenly the influencer is labeled a heretic. They seized him and made him stand trial on account of these false accusations but they saw that his face was like that of an angel. He wasn't on a marketing campaign to defend himself.

He was abiding in God's presence.

Who Do You Influence?

His final speech was his greatest moment of platform and audience reach, yet he didn't state a case for his defense. He preached truth and focused his eyes to heaven. It was in this moment Stephen saw who he was ultimately influencing (spoiler: it's not the people). He sees Jesus STANDING at the right hand of the Father (Acts 7:54-56). Stephen, influenced by Jesus's love and sacrifice sees that Jesus was INFLUENCED to stand by Stephen's love and sacrifice!

If we humble ourselves and pour out our lives for God, we too can influence the throne room of heaven! So think about this the next time you post: who are you trying to influence? Will He stand up from His throne to hear what you are saying?

— **Aletha Arkley**

As you influence, where do your motives point to? Others, yourself, or Christ?

Further Reflection

Who Do You Influence?

....
....
....
....
....
....
....
....
....
....
....
....
....
....
....
....
....
....
....
....
....
....
....
....
....
....
....
....

I'm thankful for

Lord, I'm asking you for

....

....

....

....

....

....

They chose Stephen, a man full of *faith* and of the Holy Spirit;

Acts 6:5a NIV

FIRE
Walkers

> "You yourselves are our letter, written on our hearts, known and read by everyone. You show that you are a letter from Christ, the result of our ministry, written not with ink but with the Spirit of the living God, not on tablets of stone but on tablets of human hearts."
> 2 Corinthians 3:2-3 NIV

How many of us might have sisters that feel stuck because we haven't shared what we are going through or have been through with them?

No judgement, my hand is raised!

Sometimes we use excuses like I'm shy, I'm private, I don't want to seem boastful or weak and even the "child, I don't want nobody all in my business!" But as the ones that have been pulled through the fire and not burned, how can we keep from telling them there is a way to be rescued, any longer? (Rev .12:11)

What if the Samaritan woman decided she didn't want the whole town to know that Jesus had just called her out on her stuff? (John 4:4-28)

What if the woman decided not to take the risk of worshipping at the feet of Jesus in the crowd of religious people? (Luke 7:36-48)

What if the woman with the issue of blood had just walked away instead of coming forth and admitting that she was the one that touched Jesus clothes and was healed? (Mark 5:25-34)

None of us would know the strength in overcoming habitual sin, the power of pressing in or the freedom that comes from receiving the unmerited grace and mercy of God. Although we're not jumping at the chance, we have the unique gift of having our trials, triumphs and yes, even our tragedy's serve a great purpose.

This strange but amazing privilege of walking through life and being displays of our Father's power and love is so that we can give hope to those who hear and see us.

To let them know that they are not alone. That God is the one that walks in the fire with us and will do the same for them. (2 Cor. 1:4)

So it's time, time to share you victories, time to share you sorrows and struggles, time to share your story…its already written and the world is ready to read it. (2 Cor. 3:2-3)

— April Brown

What is God stirring in your heart to share? Even now?

Further Reflection

....
....
....
....
....
....
....
....
....
....
....
....
....
....
....
....
....
....
....
....
....
....
....
....
....
....
....

I'm thankful for

Lord, I'm asking you for

....

....

....

....

....

....

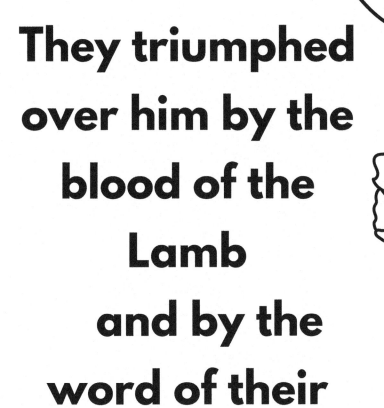

They triumphed over him by the blood of the Lamb and by the word of their

testimony

Revelations 12:11a NIV

GET COMFORTABLE BEING
Uncomfortable

> "Dear friends, I urge you, as foreigners and exiles, to abstain from sinful desires, which wage war against your soul. Live such good lives among the pagans that, though they accuse you of doing wrong, they may see your good deeds and glorify God on the day he visits us."
> 1Peter 2:11-12 NIV

There in the middle of that isometric plank —my arms shaking, my breath heavy, my whole body feeling. the. BURN. —that well-defined instructor on the other side of the television screen had the gall to say it:

"Get comfortable being uncomfortable."

Can I just be honest with you? I might have sneered as I repeated with a loud exhale, "Get comfortable being uncomfortable." I mean, that wasn't exactly the pep talk I wanted to hear at that point, but it was the pep talk that I needed to hear. My body was at odds with my mind, the former telling me to give up and the latter compelling me to muscle through it. So I chose the latter. I got comfortable being uncomfortable. After all, I knew the end result would be for my good.

And so it will be for the child of God too.

Yes, we may live IN this world, but Scripture tells us that we are not OF this world. So we should expect some level of discomfort here. And knowing that should make us think differently—not being transformed to the patterns of this world but instead renewing our minds in God's Word.

It should make us react differently—by praying for and loving our enemies instead of seeking to destroy them. It should make us speak differently—with words, as Mother Theresa says, that "give the light of Jesus" instead of "increase the darkness." It should make us care differently—by putting the needs of others before our own. It should make us love differently—with a love that always protects, always trusts, always hopes, and always perseveres.

Get Comfortable Being Uncomfortable

The Apostle Peter, like so many others, knew what it was to get comfortable being uncomfortable, exhorting us in 1 Peter 2:11-12 with these words:

"Friends, this world is not your home, so don't make yourselves cozy in it. Don't indulge your ego at the expense of your soul. Live an exemplary life among the natives so that your actions will refute their prejudices. Then they'll be won over to God's side and be there to join in the celebration when he arrives." (MSG)

So, Child of God, can I give you a pep talk? Get comfortable being uncomfortable.

— **Stephanie Prater-Clarke**

Is there something uncomfortable that God has asked you to do recently?

Further Reflection

Get Comfortable Being Uncomfortable

....
....
....
....
....
....
....
....
....
....
....
....
....
....
....
....
....
....
....
....
....
....
....
....
....
....
....

I'm thankful for

Lord, I'm asking you for

....

....

....

....

....

....

For our light
and
momentary
troubles are
achieving for
us an eternal
glory
that far
outweighs
them all.

2 Corinthians 4:17 NIV

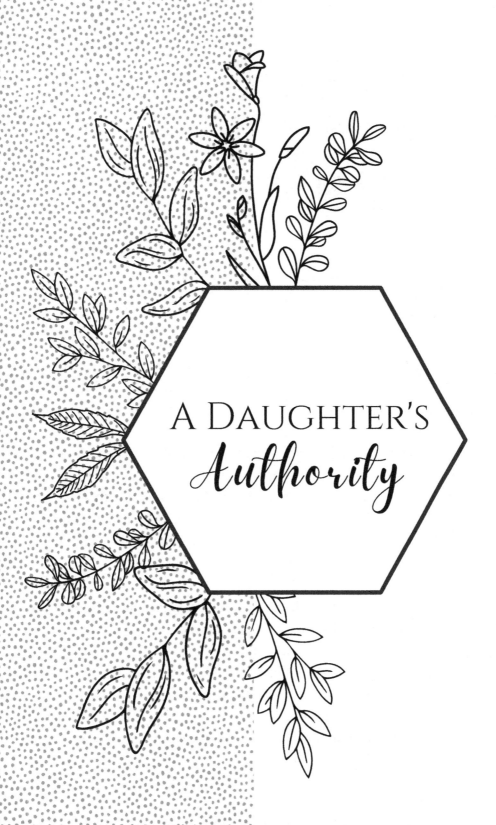

A DAUGHTER'S
Authority

> "The Spirit himself testifies with our spirit that we are God's children. Now if we are children, then we are heirs—heirs of God and co-heirs with Christ, if indeed we share in his sufferings in order that we may also share in his glory."
> Romans 8:16-17 NIV

In the book of Nehemiah we read the account of a man that knew who he was in the sight of God.

A man that obeyed God even though he faced opposition. He had a burden for his broken homeland. In the first two chapters we see that Nehemiah sought God and asked for favor with the King of Persia, so that the walls of Jerusalem could be repaired and rebuilt.

He receives this favor. He has the King's authority and blessing to go, to do the work. This included being equipped with both materials and people. Then right there, at the end of chapter two, just as the work is about to begin; right as the people of Israel have agreed to come alongside Nehemiah to do the work the King has approved; the work that God had called Nehemiah to, we see someone question it all. (Nehemiah 2:19)

These men questioned Nehemiah's calling, his strengths, his authority thru the King. It is a perfect example of what the enemy of our soul does.

Many times, we are walking out what we know God has called us to. We are beginning a ministry or business. Perhaps we are using our strengths to come alongside others in a new season. Maybe we are simply sharing the truth of God's love with those around us, and the enemy whispers to us, "What is this thing you're doing?" He tries to get us to question who we are and Whose we are.

However, our response can be the same as Nehemiah's. (Nehemiah 2:20)

A Daughter's Authority

As daughters of the King, through Jesus, we have His authority, His Spirit with us and in us. We have the authority of God to tell the enemy that he has no claim to us. He has no portion in the work we are doing. He has no right to tell us that we can not do what God has called us to do. The enemy has no authority to call us opposite of what God calls us.

God says we are His children.

He calls us good, His handiwork. He has equipped us with strengths, gifts, and people to come alongside us. Just like Nehemiah, as we are obedient in what God has called us to do, as we come into agreement with who God says we are, even in the midst of opposition, we can walk confidently forward.

— **Heidi Robidou**

How will you, from the overflow of who you are in Christ, step forward in authority?

Further Reflection

I'm thankful for

Lord, I'm asking you for

....

....

....

....

....

....

These, then, are the things you should teach. Encourage and rebuke with all

authority

Do not let anyone despise you.

Titus 2:15 NIV

SIMPLE
Obedience

> "And the God of all grace, who called you to his eternal glory in Christ, after you have suffered a little while, will himself restore you and make you strong, firm and steadfast."
> 1 Peter 5:10 NIV

When was the last time that you felt really tired?

I'm not talking about an "I didn't get enough sleep last night" tired, but an "I just don't know if I can keep doing this" kind of tired.

I have felt this kind of fatigue recently, and for the life of me I couldn't figure out what to do to fix it. A month ago, I was feeling so depleted and frustrated from trying to spread the love of God and His word, that I was ready to throw in the towel.

I have been working in vocational ministry now for almost a year with some very broken women. These women are in the very early stages of recovery from substance use disorder. The particular group that I was working with at the time were about as interested in what I had to say about Jesus as I am in hearing about anything related to numbers!

I was feeling ineffective, unheard, and like I was in the wrong place. I prayed to God that if I wasn't where I was supposed to be, doing what He wanted me to do then He needed to move me!

As I laid on my sofa after praying, I heard Him whisper this verse to me: "So let's not get tired of doing what is good. At just the right time, we will reap a harvest of blessing if we don't give up." Galatians 6:9, NLT.

I had become so focused on how these women were not receiving what I was telling them about Jesus that I lost focus on the most important thing—my obedience to God.

He gently reminded me that evening that it's not up to me to control their reactions or the outcomes when I speak to others about His word and love. That is His job. My role is simply to be obedient in telling these ladies about His pure and perfect love for them—regardless of their past.

1 Peter 5:10 tells us this: "And the God of all Grace, who called you to be his eternal glory in Christ, after you have suffered a little while, will himself restore you and make you strong, firm, and steadfast."

As you move forward in what God is asking you to do today, I encourage you to focus on obedience. HE will provide the validation you are seeking.

— Tammie Vinson

What harvest are you believing God for as you remain steadfast in "doing good"?

Further Reflection

Simple Obedience

....

....

....

....

....

....

....

....

....

....

....

....

....

....

....

....

....

....

....

....

....

....

....

....

I'm thankful for

Lord, I'm asking you for

....

....

....

....

....

....

Let us not become weary in doing good, for at the proper time we will reap a *harvest* if we do not give up.

Galatians 6:9 NIV

BEAUTY FROM
Ashes

> "to provide for those who mourn in Zion; to give them a crown of beauty instead of ashes, festive oil instead of mourning, and splendid clothes instead of despair. And they will be called righteous trees, planted by the Lord to glorify him."
> Isaiah 61:3 CSB

2020 was not the year that we imagined.

I would venture to guess that many of us would gladly set 2020 on fire, walk away with our heads held high, and let it burn to the ground. However, I want to challenge myself, and you, to reexamine our relationships with fire and reflect on the beauty that can come from the ashes. Let's take the very aspects that we hate about a fire and the struggles of the past twelve months, not to mention other countless times in our lives, and turn them into embers that burn bright and bring love, warmth, and light to others.

It seems that fires, much like life, can bring a lot of joy and a lot of pain. While purposeful fires are a thing of beauty; unexpected fires often bring destruction and despair. The patience that it takes to get that beautiful blaze of glory reminds me of the patience that we need to have with God when waiting for answers to prayer or to understand His will, His way, His purpose and His timing. Oftentimes, we are faced with fires in our lives that are smokey, smoldering, and flameless; but we must not lose sight of that fact that fires are temporary.

Fires are also useful; they destroy and eliminate the very things in our lives that are worthless. Take for example fields that are unable to produce good crops. The harvester will set the field on fire. The burning of the field is necessary to purify and restore it for its intended purpose. Friend, God uses fires in our lives for the exact same reason. He is burning away that which is not fruitful, not worthy, not productive, and He is restoring us. He consumes and destroys that which He has not planned for our lives; and His love for us, like a fire, is warm, glowing, beautiful, and consuming.

The real, true beauty and rewards of life are not instantaneous. They are the results of lighting sparks along the way and watching in wonder as God sets them ablaze. The Bible uses fire to represent God's radiant glory and the fact that His Kingdom cannot be burned. While the fires we face during our time on Earth may seem all consuming and destructive, we must remember that the dark, dingy ashes are temporary troubles. So let's keep our eyes on Jesus, the eternal flame.

— Jodi Kinasewitz

"Blessed is the man who trusts in the Lord, whose trust is the Lord. He is like a tree planted by water, that sends out its roots by the stream, and does not fear when heat comes, for its leaves remain green, and is not anxious in the year of drought, for it does not cease to bear fruit."
Jeremiah 17:7-8

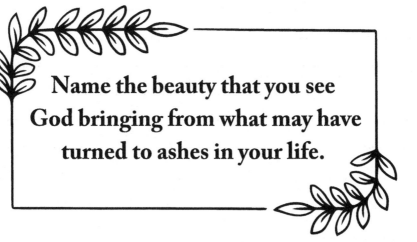

Name the beauty that you see God bringing from what may have turned to ashes in your life.

Further Reflection

I'm thankful for

Lord, I'm asking you for

....

....

....

....

....

....

But you are a chosen race, a royal priesthood, a holy nation, a people for his own possession, that you may *proclaim* the excellencies of him who called you out of darkness into his marvelous light.

1 Peter 2:9 ESV

THE CALL I
Carry

> The Lord your God is with you,
> the Mighty Warrior who saves.
> He will take great delight in you;
> in his love he will no longer rebuke you,
> but will rejoice over you with singing."
> Zephaniah 3:17 NIV

As I walk in greater truth with regard to my identity in Christ, one of my favorite passages of scripture has become Jesus' baptism by John the Baptist. The words of the Father spoken over the Son as He emerges from the waters of the Jordan River, are beautiful, affirming, encouraging and powerful. They are the words that every child wants to hear from their Father.

You are my mine. I love you. I am proud of you.

I never heard those words from an earthly father. And my heavenly Father, well...I knew He loved me. But I needed to know that His love for me was specific, not general. I knew I was His daughter, but did I really belong in the family, no matter what? Even if I never brought one single person to salvation in Christ?

Yes Dasha, you still belong! Ok, so he loved me and called me His daughter, but was He proud of me? That question was the hardest but I got an answer. He is so so unbelievably proud of me- not because of what I do or don't do. No striving needed. He is proud of me because of who I am.

I am His.

He drove this home for me over Christmas break. I was still struggling with wondering if I was doing enough. So during Christmas I did two things: I finished reading Milk and Honey and decided to watch the Hobbit trilogy. The Lord used that book and then that movie to speak powerfully to me about my identity and my purpose in this world.

The Call I Carry

The hobbits lived simply. They enjoyed life. They rested. They engaged and enjoyed fellowship with their families and community. They were the healthiest of all the races, but also thought to be the weakest. The humans, elves and dwarves, though they were mighty, seemed to be tainted by pride, arrogance, and greed.

I thought it quite revelatory that it was the weak, unassuming, simple-minded hobbits, who were chosen to save the world. The hobbits were the only race of people who were perhaps "strong" enough to carry the burden of the ring and not be completely corrupted by its evil.

I saw the value in simple living and the importance of the call that I carry. I may sometimes feel as though it's not much, but in reality I am a generational stronghold breaker. I have been set apart for the call of building a Godly marriage and family. Abandonment and brokenness will no longer be our story. My children will have a mother and father who love them and one another deeply. My children will know the value of marriage. They will have a mother who is available to love, teach, serve and guide them. They will know the peace of a home where the Lord's presence dwells. A home where the Lord's name is held high and His truths are spoken over them.

My children will grow up watching their parents be loved by the Father, Son and Holy Spirit. They will be taught the Word of God and taught to hear His voice. This is my call: to be fully loved by the Father, to give His love to my family, and to day by day build a new generation.

— Dasha Sigurmundsson

Further Reflection

The Call I Carry

....
....
....
....
....
....
....
....
....
....
....
....
....
....
....
....
....
....
....
....
....
....
....
....
....

I'm thankful for

Lord, I'm asking you for

....

....

....

....

....

....

Her teachings are
filled with

Wisdom

and kindness
as loving instruction
pours from her lips.
She watches over the
ways of her household
and meets every need
they have.

Proverbs 31:26-27 TPT

We may not think we have a place, position, or platform to impact thousands, but we have something even better. We have influence from the Holy Spirit; influence to introduce others to Jesus and influence to boast of His gospel. Daily, we encounter others in the midst of everyday work. Like us, they are running errands, making decisions, and marching through their day. God can take an encounter with one person, and impact generations with the Gospel. One encounter has the potential to reach magnitudes.

You have "ones" all around you. You may work in a boardroom, an office, a restaurant, or a shop. You may be home with your children. You may be caring for your aging parents. Each person is fully in their 'trenches" engaging in their chores and work, but we can all meet with one.

Let's look up, let's look out, and let's see the appointment He orchestrated for us to encounter. By influencing one, He will influence many. Let's trust in God that through us He will influence the many, and the one.

— Sarah Wood

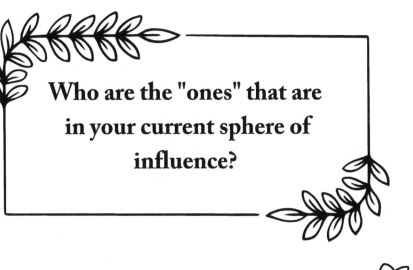

Who are the "ones" that are in your current sphere of influence?

Further Reflection

I'm thankful for

Lord, I'm asking you for

....

....

....

....

....

....

So is my *word* that goes out from my mouth: It will not return to me empty, but will accomplish what I desire and achieve the purpose for which I sent it.

Isaiah 55:11 NIV

The Authors

ALETHA ARKLEY

Aletha is a minister of the Gospel who has a passion to teach, preach, and equip the Body to do His work until His Kingdom finally comes. She is a devoted wife to Simon, and a mother to two miracle children. She currently resides in the greater Charlotte area. She was once a caged bird, but God broke the cage and gave her wings to soar.

 alethaarkley@gmail.com

APRIL BROWN

April is the proud mother of two beautiful daughters, a lover of God and all people who loves to laugh and spend time with family and friends. Her passion is to teach women how to grow in their identity in Christ, sharing the Word and love of God with everyone around her.

 facebook.com/chickery25 @itsapril_brown

STEPHANIE PRATER-CLARKE

Stephanie is a pastor's wife and a grateful mom to two teenagers. She lives in Barbados and serves alongside her husband both locally and throughout the Caribbean region. Whether it's original songs, contributing posts, or personal reflections, she has a passion to write with the hope of encouraging others. She also loves her morning walks, capturing all things creation on camera, the game of cricket, family vacations, and a good cup of coffee.

 @stephclarke Stephanie Prater Clarke

JANESSA CYPHER

Janessa is a mom of three and serves alongside her husband with Cultivate Discipleship in Northern Uganda. She has a passion to write of the beauty found in brokenness and loves to create using whatever materials she can find. However, she is more often found sipping an iced coffee while homeschooling, creating art with her kiddos or enjoying the nature surrounding their home in the African bush.

  @janessacypher Janessa Cypher ⊕ www.cdgulu.com

INFLUENCING
One

> "Many of the Samaritans from that town believed in him because of the woman's testimony, "He told me everything I ever did." John 4:39 NIV

I am currently in the trenches.

No, not the physical mud and root-filled trenches, but the trenches that a mom with three kids, 10 years old and under, finds herself in. Running here, there and everywhere with limited resources, and usually a few minutes late. Despite my full days, I know I've been called to share the gospel. As believers, we are all graced this sacred mantle and purpose. Yet, life is moving at a rapid rhythm, and there is little time to focus on myself, much less focus on the influence I have to share the Good News.

Sometimes, I feel stuck between daily life duties and the Great Commission. I want to work on a sermon, but my toddler wants me to do a puzzle. I planned to bake cookies for my neighbors and invite them to church, but I'm out of ingredients. And mercy, I should really do those dishes. There is such an extensive list of tasks in my immediate servanthood that I wonder if I will ever be in a place to focus on serving outside the home.

Last week, I read the story in the Bible of the woman at the well…the one Jesus approached and asked for a sip of water. We are astounded that Jesus spoke to her. She was a sinner, after all. But friends, let us also be astonished with the outcome of that encounter. While doing an everyday chore on a seemingly ordinary day, a woman met the Savior. She inherited eternal life and a relationship with The Father through her faith. Then she raced to her hometown to share of her impromptu meeting with Jesus. Scripture says "many" believed as a result of her testimony. She had influence that was anointed by Jesus Christ. To put it in a nutshell, an encounter with one, influenced many.

ASHLEY DJOKOTO

Ashley is a wife, teacher, and cross-cultural worker. She and her husband live in the capital of Ghana. She loves reading, calligraphy art, deep conversations with friends, and writing all kinds of things.

🌐 https://fromatlantatoaccra.wordpress.com

ERIN ELISE

Erin is a writer, photographer, and inspirational speaker.
She is also the founder of Affirmed Candle Collection.
Find out more on her website Just Love Thyself.

🌐 www.justlovethyself.com

JODI KINASEWITZ

Jodi is a wife to her husband Matt and a mother to their four children. She is also an elementary level Reading specialist and a certified yoga instructor. She is passionate about leading Christian inspired yoga classes, reading, and writing. She loves to travel with her family, and she spends any time she can outdoors.

📷 @jkinasewitz   f jodi.kinasewitz   🌐 jkinasewitz.wixsite.com/website

NAOMI MARKLEW

Naomi Marklew is a writer living in Durham in the North East of England with her husband and two sons. She has poetry and prose in various online and print publications, and is currently working on a book about Devotional Creativity, which will include both theological material and practical creative prompts. She is also the Durham Branch Leader for the UK's Christian Creative Network.

🐦 @NaomiMarklew   f https://www.facebook.com/naomi.marklew
🌐 naomimarklew.wixsite.com/website | christiancreativenetwork.com

The Authors

RACHEL MUTESI

Rachel has a heart for people to hear the Good News of Jesus Christ, especially for those who have never had the opportunity to hear of Him before. Outside of her work in a university ministry in Australia, Rachel enjoys a good cup of tea, stories, writing, exploring new places and has just discovered painting.

🌐 https://thisgloriousadventure.wordpress.com

TOYA POPLAR

Toya Poplar is an author and connection coach who encourages women to take care of the caretaker. You can find her latest book Black Pearls on Amazon, or connect with her by joining her self-care group, Wifey Presents: Black Pearls Facebook Community.

 @BlackPearlsBook toyapoplar.com

RUTH POTINU

Ruth Potinu works alongside her husband in Papua New Guinea where they seek to minister to the vulnerable, especially widows and their children. She loves a good cup of chai, spending time with her busy kiddos and writing whenever she can carve out the time.

 @ruthpotinu facebook.com/ruth.uehle
🌐 www.simplycontemplating.wordpress.com

HEIDI L. ROBIDOU

Heidi L. Robidou is a proud Mrs. and boy mom who calls Kansas home. She enjoys writing about the everyday glimpses of glory seen and lessons learned here on earth. Heidi has a passion for ministering to women through encouragement, with prayer, and by pointing them to the truth of God's Word.

 @HeidiLRobidou

DASHA SIGURMUNDSSON

Dasha was born and raised in Florence, Alabama but has lived in Huntsville, Alabama for the last 23 years. She is passionate about good food, her family, and Jesus!

 Dsigurmundsson@gmail.com @dashasigurmundsson

TAMMIE VINSON

Tammie is a wife to her husband Lawrence and mom to 2 children. She serves as a women's ministry leader as well as a chaplain to women recovering from substance use disorder. She enjoys traveling, writing, reading, good coffee, being outdoors, and yoga.

 @tvinson1124

SARAH WOOD

Sarah Wood is a follower of Jesus, wife to Sam, mama to 3, an author, and the Editor in Chief of Mom Mentor. She spends her free days reading, biking in the sunshine, or at the beach with an ice coffee. She is fiercely passionate about the grace-filled Gospel of Jesus and sharing the love and truth of God.

 @sarahwoodwrites www.mommentor.org

BUFFI YOUNG

Buffi is a wife to her best friend for over 26 years and a mom to 4 amazing children. She and her husband have a heart for adoption and strengthening families, have authored a children's book about their adoption story, and developed hands-on family devotions. Buffi has a heart to encourage others through written communication and desires to help other women see themselves through God's eyes!

⊕ miracle.markandbuffi.com | grafted.markandbuffi.com
www.pearlsofpurpose.blogspot.com | www.piecesofthepromise.com

About

JENNY ERLINGSSON | MILK & HONEY BOOKS

Jenny is the founder of Milk & Honey Women and Milk & Honey Books, where she encourages others to remain firmly rooted in Christ, stir the gifts of God within them and step confidently into their God-breathed purposes. Jenny is the author of books and resources including, Becoming His and Milk & Honey in the Land of Fire & Ice. She and her husband live and minister in Iceland with their four equally cute and feisty children.

She is so thankful to feature the voices of these women in this devotional journal and would like to give special thanks to Sarah Wood for her help with edits. If you are interested in submitting content for a future project or for the following blogs, head over to the sites below to sign up for the email list.

 @jennyerlingsson   jennyerlingsson.com | fireandicefamily.com

Encouraging women to cultivate Christ-Centered Identity, Intimacy & Influence in every season.

  @milkandhoneywomen   milkandhoneywomen.com

Encouraging Writers, Releasing Creative Resources, & Publishing uplifting, Christ-Centered books.

  @milkandhoneybooks   milkandhoneybooks.com

Made in the USA
Las Vegas, NV
26 April 2021